BILL GATES

BIOGRAPHY : LIFE FROM BEGINNING TO END

TEAM INDUS

ISBN 979-888530192-3

Contents

Preface

William Henry Gates III (conceived October 28, 1955) is an American business financier, programming engineer, financial backer, creator, and altruist. He is a fellow benefactor of Microsoft, alongside his late cherished companion Paul Allen.[2][3] During his vocation at Microsoft, Gates stood firm on the footholds of administrator, (CEO), president and boss programming modeler, while likewise being the biggest individual investor until May 2014.[4] He is viewed as one of the most amazing known business visionaries of the microcomputer transformation of the 1970s and 1980s.

Entryways was brought up in Seattle, Washington. In 1975, he and Allen established Microsoft in Albuquerque, New Mexico. It turned into the world's biggest PC programming company.[5][a] Gates drove the organization as administrator and CEO until venturing down as CEO in January 2000, prevailed by Steve Ballmer, however he remained executive of the directorate and became boss programming architect.[8] During the last part of the 1990s, he was condemned for his business strategies, which have been viewed as hostile to cutthroat. This assessment has been maintained by various court rulings.[9] In June 2008, Gates progressed to low maintenance job at Microsoft and regular employment at the Bill and Melinda Gates Foundation, the private beneficent establishment he and his then-spouse, Melinda Gates, set up in 2000.[10] He ventured down as administrator of the leading body of Microsoft in February 2014 and accepted another post as innovation counsel to help the recently delegated CEO Satya Nadella.[11] In March 2020, Gates left his board positions at Microsoft and Berkshire Hathaway to zero in on his generous endeavors including environmental change, worldwide wellbeing and advancement, and education.[12]

Starting around 1987, Gates has been remembered for the Forbes rundown of the world's most affluent people.[13][14] From 1995 to 2017, he held the Forbes title of the most extravagant individual on the planet consistently besides from 2010 to 2013.[15] In October 2017, he was outperformed by Amazon originator and CEO Jeff Bezos, who had an expected total assets of US$90.6 billion contrasted with Gates' total assets of US$89.9 billion at the time.[16] As of October 2021, Gates had an expected total assets of US$129 billion, making him the fourth-most extravagant individual in the world.[17]

Later in his vocation and since passing on everyday tasks at Microsoft in 2008, Gates has sought after numerous business and humanitarian undertakings. He is the author and executive of a few organizations, including BEN, Cascade Investment, bgC3, and TerraPower. He has given sizable measures of cash to different altruistic associations and logical examination programs through the Bill and Melinda Gates Foundation, answered to be the world's biggest private charity.[18] Through the establishment, he drove a mid 21st century immunization crusade which essentially added to the destruction of the wild poliovirus in Africa.[19][20] In 2010, Gates and Warren Buffett established The Giving Pledge, by which they and different very rich people vow to give half of their abundance to philanthropy.[21]

CHAPTER ONE

Early Life

> "*"If you can't make it good, at least make it look good."*"

Charge Gates was brought into the world in Seattle, Washington on October 28, 1955.[3] He is the child of William H. Entryways Sr.[b] (1925–2020) and Mary Maxwell Gates (1929–1994).[22] His lineage incorporates English, German, and Irish/Scots-Irish.[23] His dad was a noticeable legal counselor, and his mom served on the governing body for First Interstate BancSystem and the United Way of America. Doors' maternal granddad was J. W. Maxwell, a public bank president. Doors has a more seasoned sister Kristi (Kristianne) and a more youthful sister Libby. He is the fourth of his name in his family however is known as William Gates III or "Three pointer" (i.e., three) since his dad had the "II" suffix.[24][25] The family resided in the Sand Point space of Seattle in a home that was harmed by an uncommon twister when Gates was seven years old.[26]

Right off the bat in his life, Gates saw that his folks needed him to seek after a law career.[27] When he was youthful, his family routinely went to a congregation of the

Congregational Christian Churches, a Protestant Reformed denomination.[28][29][30] Gates was little for his age and was tormented as a child.[25] The family energized contest; one guest revealed that "it didn't make any difference whether it was hearts or pickleball or swimming to the dock; there was consistently a prize for winning and there was consistently a punishment for losing".[31]

Entryways (right) with Paul Allen at Lakeside School in 1970 At 13, he selected the private Lakeside prep school,[32][33] where he composed his first programming program.[34] When he was in the eighth grade, the Mothers' Club at the school utilized returns from Lakeside School's scrounge deal to purchase a Teletype Model 33 ASR terminal and a square of PC time on a General Electric (GE) PC for the students.[35] Gates looked into programming the GE framework in BASIC, and he was pardoned from math classes to seek after his advantage. He composed his first PC program on this machine, an execution of spasm tac-toe that permitted clients to mess around against the PC. Entryways was intrigued by the machine and how it would consistently execute programming code perfectly.[36] After the Mothers Club gift was depleted, Gates and different understudies looked for time on frameworks including DEC PDP minicomputers. One of these frameworks was a PDP-10 having a place with Computer Center Corporation (CCC) which restricted Gates, Paul Allen, Ric Weiland, and Gates' closest companion and first colleague Kent Evans, for the mid year after it found them taking advantage of bugs in the working framework to get free PC time.[37][25]

The four understudies framed the Lakeside Programmers Club to make money.[25] At the finish of the boycott, they proposed to observe bugs in CCC's product in return for additional PC time. Rather than utilizing the framework remotely by means of Teletype, Gates went to CCC's workplaces and read up source code for different projects that ran on the framework, including Fortran, Lisp, and machine language. The course of action with CCC proceeded until 1970 when the organization left business.

The next year, a Lakeside instructor enrolled Gates and Evans to mechanize the school's class-planning framework, giving them PC time and sovereignties consequently. The couple worked determinedly to have the program prepared for their senior year. Towards the finish of their lesser year, Evans was killed in a hiking mishap, which Gates has depicted as probably the saddest day of his life. Doors then, at that point, gone to Allen who assisted him with completing the framework for Lakeside.[25]

At 17, Gates framed an endeavor with Allen called Traf-O-Data to make traffic counters dependent on the Intel 8008 processor.[38] In 1972, he filled in as a legislative page in the House of Representatives.[39][40] He was a National Merit Scholar when he moved on from Lakeside School in 1973.[41] He scored 1590 out of 1600 on the Scholastic Aptitude Tests (SAT) and selected at Harvard College in the fall of 1973.[42][43] He picked a pre-law major however took arithmetic and graduate level software engineering courses.[44] While at Harvard, he met individual understudy Steve Ballmer. Entryways left Harvard following two years while Ballmer remained and graduated magna cum laude. A long time later, Ballmer succeeded Gates as Microsoft's CEO and kept up with that situation from 2000 until his acquiescence in 2014.[45][46]

Entryways concocted a calculation for flapjack arranging as an answer for one of a progression of perplexing problems[47] introduced in a combinatorics class by teacher Harry Lewis. His answer held the record as the quickest form for north of 30 years, and its replacement is quicker by just 2%.[47][48] His answer was formalized and distributed as a team with Harvard PC researcher Christos Papadimitriou.[49]

Doors kept in touch with Paul Allen and went along with him at Honeywell throughout the late spring of 1974.[50] In 1975, the MITS Altair 8800 was delivered dependent on the Intel 8080 CPU, and Gates and Allen saw the chance to begin their own program company.[51] Gates exited Harvard that very year. His folks were strong of him in the wake of perceiving the amount he needed to begin his own company.[52] He disclosed his choice to leave Harvard: "assuming that things hadn't worked out, I could generally return to school. I was formally on leave."[53]

CHAPTER TWO

Story of Success

> *"Success is a lousy teacher. It seduces smart people into thinking they can't lose."*

Doors read the January 1975 issue of Popular Electronics which showed the Altair 8800, and he reached Micro Instrumentation and Telemetry Systems (MITS) to illuminate them that he and others were chipping away at a BASIC mediator for the platform.[54] truly, Gates and Allen didn't have an Altair and had not composed code for it; they simply needed to measure MITS's advantage. MITS president Ed Roberts consented to meet them for an exhibit, and throughout the span of half a month they fostered an Altair emulator that ran on a minicomputer, and afterward the BASIC translator. The exhibition was held at MITS's workplaces in Albuquerque, New Mexico; it was a triumph and brought about an arrangement with MITS to circulate the translator as Altair BASIC. MITS employed Allen,[55] and Gates withdrew from nonappearance from Harvard to work with him at MITS in November 1975. Allen named their association "Miniature Soft", a blend of "microcomputer" and "programming", and their first office was in Albuquerque. The main representative Gates and

Allen recruited was their secondary school teammate Ric Weiland.[55] They dropped the dash inside a year and formally enrolled the trademark "Microsoft" with the Secretary of the State of New Mexico on November 26, 1976.[55] Gates always avoided Harvard to finish his examinations.

Microsoft's Altair BASIC was famous with PC specialists, however Gates found that a pre-market duplicate had spilled out and was as a rule broadly replicated and disseminated. In February 1976, he composed an Open Letter to Hobbyists in the MITS bulletin in which he declared that over 90% of the clients of Microsoft Altair BASIC had not paid Microsoft for itself and the Altair "side interest market" was at risk for killing the motivating force for any expert designers to deliver, disperse, and keep up with great software.[56] This letter was disagreeable with numerous PC specialists, however Gates endured in his conviction that product engineers ought to have the option to request installment. Microsoft became autonomous of MITS in late 1976, and it kept on creating programming language programming for different systems.[55] The organization moved from Albuquerque to Bellevue, Washington on January 1, 1979.[54]

Doors said he by and by audited and regularly revised each line of code that the organization created in its initial five years. As the organization developed, he changed into a director job, then, at that point, an executive.[57]

DONKEY.BAS, is a PC game written in 1981 and included with early forms of the PC DOS working framework dispersed with the first IBM PC. It is a driving game where the player should try not to hit jackasses. The game was composed by Gates and Neil Konzen.[58][59]

IBM, the main provider of PC hardware to business endeavors at that point, moved toward Microsoft in July 1980 concerning programming for its impending PC, the IBM PC,[60] after Bill Gates' mom, Mary Maxwell Gates, referenced Microsoft to John Opel, IBM's CEO.[61] IBM previously suggested that Microsoft compose the BASIC translator. IBM's agents additionally referenced that they required a working framework, and Gates alluded them to Digital Research (DRI), producers of the broadly utilized CP/M working system.[62] IBM's conversations with Digital Research went ineffectively, nonetheless, and they didn't agree. IBM agent Jack Sams referenced the permitting hardships during an ensuing gathering with Gates and inquired as to whether Microsoft could give a working framework. Half a month after the fact, Gates and Allen proposed utilizing 86-DOS, a working framework like CP/M, that Tim Paterson of Seattle Computer Products (SCP) had made for equipment like the PC.[63] Microsoft made an arrangement with SCP to be the selective permitting specialist of 86-DOS, and later the full proprietor. Microsoft utilized Paterson to adjust the working framework for the PC[64] and conveyed it to IBM as PC DOS for a one-time frame expense of $50,000.[65]

The actual agreement just procured Microsoft a moderately little expense. It was the renown brought to Microsoft by IBM's reception of their working framework that would be the beginning of Microsoft's change from an independent venture to the main programming organization on the planet. Entryways had not proposed to move the copyright on the working framework to IBM in light of the fact that he accepted that other PC producers would clone IBM's PC hardware.[65] They did, making the IBM-viable PC, running DOS, a true norm. The deals of MS-

DOS (the adaptation of DOS offered to clients other than IBM) made Microsoft a key part in the industry.[66] The press immediately recognized Microsoft as being extremely powerful on the IBM PC. PC Magazine inquired as to whether Gates was "the man behind the machine?".[60]

Entryways managed Microsoft's organization rebuilding on June 25, 1981, which re-consolidated the organization in Washington state and made Gates the president and executive of the board, with Paul Allen as VP and bad habit administrator. In mid 1983, Allen left the organization in the wake of getting a Hodgkin lymphoma analysis, adequately finishing the proper business association among Gates and Allen, which had been stressed a long time earlier because of a combative argument about Microsoft equity.[54][67] Later in the decade, Gates fixed his relationship with Allen and together the two gave millions to their youth school Lakeside.[25] They remained companions until Allen's passing in October 2018.[68]

Microsoft and Gates dispatched their first retail form of Microsoft Windows on November 20, 1985, trying to fight off contest from Apple's Macintosh GUI, which had entranced buyers without any difficulty of use.[69] In August of the next year, the organization hit an arrangement with IBM to foster a different working framework called OS/2. Albeit the two organizations effectively fostered the primary adaptation of the new framework, the association decayed because of mounting imaginative differences.[70] The working framework outgrew DOS in a natural manner more than 10 years, until with Windows 95 the DOS text screen was consigned to the storeroom. Windows XP, delivered one year after Gates ventured down as Microsoft CEO, allegedly was the first to not be founded on DOS.[71] Windows 8.1 was the last form of the OS delivered before Gates passed on the seat of the firm to John W. Thompson on February 5, 2014.[72] As of 2021, the most recent arrival of the OS is known as Windows 11.

Doors had essential obligation regarding Microsoft's item procedure from the organization's establishing from 1975 until 2006. He acquired a standing for being far off from others; an industry chief whined in 1981 that "Doors is famous for not being reachable by telephone and for not returning telephone calls."[73] An Atari leader reviewed that he showed Gates a game and crushed him 35 of multiple times. At the point when they met again a month after the fact, Gates "won or tied each game. He had concentrated on the game until he addressed it. That is a competitor".[74]

In the mid 1980s, while colleague Paul Allen was going through therapies for disease, Gates — as indicated by Allen — contrived to decrease Allen's portion in Microsoft by giving himself stock options.[75][76][77] In his personal history, Allen would later review that Gates was "plotting to scam me. It was hired fighter advantage plain and simple".[75] Gates says he recollects the scene differently.[76] Allen would likewise review that Gates was inclined to yelling episodes.[77]

Entryways met consistently with Microsoft's ranking directors and program supervisors, and the chiefs depicted him as being verbally confrontational. He likewise upbraided them for saw openings in their business techniques or recommendations that set the organization's drawn out interests at risk.[78][79] He intruded on introductions with so much remarks as "that is the dumbest thing I've ever heard"[80] and "how about you simply surrender your choices and join the Peace Corps?"[81] The objective of his eruption would then need to guard the proposition exhaustively until Gates was completely convinced.[80] When subordinates gave off an impression of being dawdling, he was known to comment mockingly, "I'll do it over the weekend."[82][83][84] Gates has been blamed for harassing Microsoft employees.[85]

During Microsoft's initial years, Gates was a functioning programming engineer, especially in the organization's modifying language items, however his essential job in the vast majority of the organization's set of experiences was as a chief and leader. He has not authoritatively been in an advancement group since chipping away at the TRS-80 Model 100,[86] yet he composed code that delivered with the organization's items as late as 1989.[83] Jerry Pournelle wrote in 1985 when Gates reported Microsoft Excel: "Bill Gates loves the program, not on the grounds that it will make him huge amount of cash (in spite of the fact that I'm certain it will do that), but since it's a flawless hack."[87]

On June 15, 2006, Gates declared that he would progress out of his job at Microsoft to commit more opportunity to charity. He continuously split his obligations between two replacements when he set Ray Ozzie accountable for the board and Craig Mundie responsible for long haul item strategy.[88] The cycle required two years to completely move his obligations to Ozzie and Mundie, and was finished on June 27, 2008.[89]

Entryways supported numerous choices that prompted antitrust prosecution over Microsoft's strategic approaches. In the 1998 United States v. Microsoft case, Gates gave statement declaration that few columnists portrayed as equivocal. He contended with inspector David Boies over the relevant significance of words, for example, "contend", "concerned", and "we". Later in the year, when parts of the recorded affidavit were played back in court, the appointed authority was seen giggling and shaking his head.[90] BusinessWeek announced:

Early adjusts of his testimony show him offering obfuscatory answers and saying "I don't remember" so often that even the managing judge needed to laugh. More terrible, a large number of the innovation boss' disavowals and supplications of obliviousness were straightforwardly discredited by investigators with pieces of email that Gates both sent and received.[91]

Entryways later said that he had just opposed endeavors by Boies to misrepresent his words and activities. "Did I fence with Boies? ... I concede ... impoliteness to Boies in the first degree."[92] Despite Gates' refusals, the adjudicator decided that Microsoft had submitted imposing business model, tying and impeding contest, each disregarding the Sherman Antitrust Act.[92]

CHAPTER THREE

After Microsoft

> *"I really had a lot of dreams when I was a kid, and I think a great deal of that grew out of the fact that I had a chance to read a lot."*

Since passing on everyday tasks at Microsoft, Gates has proceeded with his generosity and chips away at different activities. As indicated by the Bloomberg Billionaires Index, Gates was the world's most noteworthy procuring tycoon in 2013, as his total assets expanded by US$15.8 billion to US$78.5 billion. As of January 2014, a large portion of Gates' resources are held in Cascade Investment LLC, a substance through which he possesses stakes in various organizations, including Four Seasons Hotels and Resorts, and Corbis Corp.[93] On February 4, 2014, Gates ventured down as executive of Microsoft to turn into "innovation consultant" at the firm, close by CEO Satya Nadella.[11][94]

Doors gave his viewpoint on a scope of issues in a generous meeting that was distributed in the March 27, 2014 issue of Rolling Stone magazine. In the meeting, Gates gave his point of view on environmental change, his magnanimous exercises, different tech organizations and individuals associated with them, and the territory of America. In light of an inquiry concerning his biggest dread when he looks 50 years into the future, Gates expressed: "there'll be some genuinely terrible things that will occur in the following 50 or 100 years, yet ideally not a solitary one of them on the size of, say, 1,000,000 individuals that you didn't anticipate dieing from a pandemic, or atomic or bioterrorism." Gates likewise distinguished development as the "genuine driver of progress" and articulated that "America's way preferable today over it's ever been."[95]

Doors has communicated worry about the likely damages of genius; in a Reddit "ask me anything", he expressed that:

First the machines will do a great deal of occupations for ourselves and not be hyper-genius. That ought to be positive assuming we oversee it well. Years and years after that however the knowledge is sufficiently able to be a worry. I concur with Elon Musk and some others on this and fail to see the reason why certain individuals are not concerned.

In a meeting that was held at the TED gathering in March 2015, with Baidu's CEO, Robin Li, Gates said he would "energetically suggest" Nick Bostrom's new work, Superintelligence: Paths, Dangers, Strategies.[100] During the meeting, Gates cautioned that the world was not ready for the following pandemic, a circumstance that would happen in late 2019 when the COVID-19 pandemic began.[101] In March 2018, Gates met at his home in Seattle with Mohammed canister Salman, the reformist crown sovereign and accepted leader of Saudi Arabia to examine venture openings for Saudi Vision 2030.[102][103] In June 2019, Gates conceded that losing the versatile working framework rush to Android was his greatest error. He expressed that it was inside their range of abilities of being the predominant player, however somewhat faults the antitrust case during the time.[104] That very year, Gates turned into a warning load up individual from the Bloomberg New Economy Forum.[105]

On March 13, 2020, Microsoft reported Gates would leave his load up positions at Berkshire Hathaway and Microsoft to commit his endeavors in humanitarian undertakings, for example, environmental change, worldwide wellbeing and improvement, and education.[12]

During the COVID-19 pandemic, Gates has generally been taken a gander at by news sources as a specialist on the issue, in spite of him not being a public authority or having any earlier clinical training.[106] His establishment did, nonetheless, build up the COVID-19 Therapeutics Accelerator in 2020 to hurry the turn of events and assessment of new and repurposed medications and biologics to treat patients for COVID-19,[107] and, as of February 2021, Gates communicated that he and Anthony Fauci regularly talk and team up on issues including immunizations and other clinical developments to battle the pandemic.[108]

Undertakings and speculations (fractional rundown) Doors has a multi-billion dollar speculation portfolio with stake in different sectors[109] and has taken part in a few enterprising endeavors past Microsoft, including:

AutoNation, car retailer that Gates has a 16% stake in exchanging on the NYSE.[citation needed] bgC3 LLC, a research organization and think-tank established by Gates.[citation needed] Canadian National Railway (CN), a Canadian Class I cargo rail route. Starting at 2019, Gates is the biggest single investor of CN stock.[110] Course Investment LLC, a private venture and holding organization consolidated in the United States, established and constrained by Gates and settled in Kirkland, Washington.[citation needed] Entryways is the top private proprietor of farmland in the United States with landholdings possessed through Cascade Investment totalling 242,000 sections of land across 19 states.[111][112] He is the 49th biggest private proprietor of land in the US.[113] Carbon Engineering, a revenue driven endeavor established by David Keith, which Gates helped fund.[114][115][116] It's is additionally upheld by Chevron Corporation and Occidental Petroleum.[117]

SCoPEx, Keith's scholarly endeavor in "sun-darkening" geoengineering, which Gates gave a large portion of the $12 million for.[118] Corbis (initially named Interactive Home Systems and presently known as Branded Entertainment Network), a computerized picture permitting and freedoms administrations organization established and led by Gates.[119] EarthNow, Seattle-based new business expecting to cover the Earth with live satellite video inclusion. Doors is a huge monetary backer.[120] Obscure Aviation, an old producer of extremely light planes. Doors was a significant partner from the beginning in the project.[citation needed] Unthinkable Foods, an organization that creates plant-based substitutes for meat items. A portion of the $396 million Patrick O. Brown gathered for his business came from Gates around 2014 to 2017.[121][122][123] Ecolab, worldwide supplier of water, cleanliness and energy advances and administrations to the food, energy, medical services, modern and accommodation markets. Joined with the offers claimed by the Foundation, Gates possesses 11.6% of the organization. An investor arrangement in 2012 permitted him to take ownership of 25% of the organization, yet this understanding was removed.[124]

ResearchGate, a long range informal communication site for researchers. Doors took part in a $35 million round of financing alongside other investors.[125] TerraPower, an atomic reactor configuration organization helped to establish and led by Gates, which is creating cutting edge voyaging wave reactor thermal energy stations with an end goal to handle environment change.[126][127][128][129][130] Advancement Energy Ventures, a shut asset for affluent people who look for ROI on a 20-year skyline (see next area), which "is subsidizing green new companies and a large group of other low-carbon enterprising undertakings, including everything from cutting edge atomic innovation to manufactured bosom milk." It was established by Gates in 2015.[131] Ginkgo Bioworks, a biotech startup that got $350 million in adventure financing in 2019, partially from Gates' trading company Cascade Investment.[132] Iridescent Computing, an organization that creates neuromorphic photonic incorporated circuits for AI speed increase. Mologic, British symptomatic innovation organization that Gates bought, alongside the Soros Economic Development Fund, "which has created 10-minute Covid sidelong stream tests that it plans to make for just $1."[133]

Doors considers environmental change and worldwide admittance to energy to be basic, interrelated issues. He has encouraged legislatures and the private area to put resources into innovative work to make spotless, solid energy less expensive. Doors imagines that an advancement development in supportable energy innovation could drive down both ozone harming substance discharges and neediness, and bring financial advantages by balancing out energy prices.[134] In 2011, he said: "In case you gave me the decision between picking the following 10 presidents or guaranteeing that energy is harmless to the ecosystem and a quarter as expensive, I'd pick the energy thing."[135]

In 2015, he expounded on the test of progressing the world's energy framework from one dependent on petroleum products to one dependent on supportable energy sources. Worldwide energy advances have generally required many years. He expressed, "I accept we can make this change quicker, both in light of the fact that the speed of development is speeding up, and in light of the fact that we have never had such an earnest motivation to move from one wellspring of energy to another."[136] This fast progress, as indicated by Gates, would rely upon expanded government subsidizing for fundamental exploration and monetarily hazardous private-area venture, to empower advancement in different regions like thermal power, matrix energy stockpiling to work with more prominent utilization of sunlight based and wind energy, and sun based fuels.[137]

The European Commission, European Investment Bank and Gates' Breakthrough Energy Catalyst concurred at the 2021 UN Climate Change gathering to cooperate to put up green innovations for sale to the public. Doors led two drives that he reported at the 2015 United Nations Climate Change Conference in Paris. One was Mission Innovation, in which 20 public legislatures swore to twofold their spending on innovative work for without carbon energy in more than five years' time.[134] Another drive was Breakthrough Energy, a gathering of financial backers who consented to support high hazard new companies in clean energy advancements.

Entryways, who had as of now contributed $1 billion of his own cash in imaginative energy new companies, submitted a further $1 billion to Breakthrough Energy.[137] In December 2020, he required the U.S. central government to make organizations for clean energy research, comparable to the National Institutes of Health.[138] Gates has additionally asked rich countries to move to 100% manufactured meat enterprises to diminish ozone depleting substance outflows from food production.[139]

Entryways has been condemned for holding a huge stake in Signature Aviation, an organization that administrations emanations concentrated private jets.[140] In 2019, he started to strip from petroleum derivatives. He doesn't anticipate that divestment itself should have a lot of reasonable effect, however says that assuming his endeavors to give options were to fizzle, he would not have any desire to actually profit from an increment in petroleum derivative stock prices.[141] After distributing his book How to Avoid a Climate Disaster, portions of the environment dissident local area scrutinized Gate's methodology as innovative solutionism.[142]

In June 2021, Gates' organization TerraPower and Warren Buffett's PacifiCorp reported the main Sodium atomic reactor in Wyoming. Wyoming Governor Mike Gordon hailed the task as a stage toward carbon-negative atomic power. Wyoming Senator John Barrasso likewise said that it could help the state's once dynamic uranium mining industry.[143]

In 1998, Gates dismissed the requirement for guideline of the product business in declaration before the United States Senate.[144] During the Federal Trade Commission's (FTC) examination of Microsoft during the

1990s, Gates was allegedly resentful about Commissioner Dennis Yao for "float[ing] a line of speculative inquiries recommending potential checks on Microsoft's developing syndication power". As indicated by one source: Doors was vexed. "He began by calling Yao's thoughts communist," reviews a source acquainted with the July 15 gathering, "and as he got progressively an and progressively loud, he got into calling them Communistic.

On February 18, 2021, after Facebook and Twitter had prohibited Donald Trump from their foundation because of the 2020 United States official political decision which prompted the 2021 United States Capitol assault, Gates said a super durable boycott of Trump "would be a disgrace" and would be an "drastic action". He cautioned that it would cause "polarization" in case clients with various political perspectives split among different informal communities, and said: "I don't think forbidding someone who really got a reasonable number of votes (in the official political decision) – well under a greater part – however I don't think having him off everlastingly would be that good."[144]

In April 2021, during the COVID-19 pandemic, Gates was censured for recommending that drug organizations should clutch licenses for COVID-19 immunizations. The analysis came because of the chance of this keeping more unfortunate countries from getting satisfactory immunizations. Tara Van Ho of the University of Essex expressed, "Doors talks as though every one of the lives being lost in India are inescapable however ultimately the West will help when truly the US and UK are holding their feet on the neck of creating states by declining to break [intellectual property rights] securities. It's disgusting."[146]

CHAPTER FOUR

Philantropy

"“Your most unhappy customers are your greatest source of learning.”"

Doors concentrated on crafted by Andrew Carnegie and John D. Rockefeller, and gave a portion of his Microsoft stock in 1994 to make the "William H. Entryways Foundation". In 2000, Gates and his better half consolidated three family establishments and Gates gave stock esteemed at $5 billion to make the magnanimous Bill and Melinda Gates Foundation, which was recognized by the Funds for NGOs organization in 2013, as the world's richest altruistic establishment, with resources apparently esteemed at more than $34.6 billion.[147][148] The establishment permits supporters to get to data that shows how its cash is being spent, not normal for other major beneficent associations, for example, the Wellcome Trust.[149][150] Gates, through his establishment, additionally gave $20 million to Carnegie Mellon University for another structure to be named Gates Center for Computer Science which opened in 2009.

Entryways has credited the liberality and broad magnanimity of David Rockefeller as a significant impact.

Entryways and his dad met with Rockefeller a few times, and their foundation work is halfway demonstrated on the Rockefeller family's altruistic concentration, by which they are keen on handling the worldwide issues that are overlooked by state run administrations and other organizations.[153] As of 2007, Bill and Melinda Gates were the second-most liberal donors in America, having given more than $28 billion to charity;[154] the couple plan to ultimately give 95% of their abundance to charity.[155]

The establishment is coordinated into five program regions: Global Development Division, Global Health Division, United States Division, and Global Policy and Advocacy Division. Among others, it upholds a wide scope of general wellbeing projects, allowing help to battle contagious infections such AIDS, tuberculosis and jungle fever, just as far and wide antibody projects to annihilate polio. It awards assets to learning organizations and libraries and supports grants at colleges. The establishment set up a water, sterilization and cleanliness program to give reasonable disinfection administrations in poor countries.[156] Its horticulture division upholds the International Rice Research Institute in creating Golden Rice, a hereditarily adjusted rice variation used to battle nutrient A deficiency.[157] The objective of the establishment is to give 120 million ladies and young ladies, in the least fortunate nations, with great preventative data and administrations, with the more drawn out term objective of general admittance to deliberate family planning.[158] In 2007, the Los Angeles Times condemned the establishment for putting its resources in organizations that have been blamed for deteriorating destitution, contamination and drug firms that don't offer to creating countries.[159] Although the establishment declared an audit of its ventures to evaluate social responsibility,[160] it was accordingly dropped and maintained its strategy of contributing for most extreme return, while utilizing casting a ballot rights to impact organization practices.[161]

Doors in a fireside visit directed by Shereen Bhan practically at the Singapore FinTech Festival 2020. Doors conveyed his contemplations in a fireside talk directed by writer and reporter Shereen Bhan basically at the Singapore FinTech Festival on December 8, 2020, on the theme, "Building Infrastructure for Resilience: What the COVID-19 Response Can Teach Us About How to Scale Financial Inclusion".[162]

States are there to think ahead to terrible things that may occur. On account of (the Covid-19) pandemic, insufficient was finished. We can't fail to remember that another pandemic will come and we'll have to put resources into being prepared in that, ... while not failing to remember that we were not ready and we must contribute - very much like having a local group of fire-fighters - some cash wisely and really reproduce what may occur and ensure that we're prepared for it.[162] Entryways inclines toward the standardization of COVID-19 veils. In a November 2020 meeting, he said: "How are these, similar to, nudists? That is to say, you know, we request that you wear pants, and no American says, or not very many Americans say, that that is, similar to, some horrible thing."[163]

Melinda Gates proposed that individuals ought to copy the humanitarian endeavors of the Salwen family, who sold their home and parted with half of its worth, as itemized in their book, The Power of Half.[164] Gates and his significant other welcomed Joan Salwen to Seattle to talk regarding what the family had done, and on December 9, 2010, Bill and Melinda Gates and financial backer Warren Buffett each marked a responsibility they called the "Giving Pledge", which is a responsibility by every one of the three to give to some degree half of their abundance, throughout the process of things working out, to charity.[165][166][167]

Entryways has likewise given individual gifts to instructive establishments. In 1999, Gates gave $20 million to the Massachusetts Institute of Technology for the development of a PC research facility named the "William H. Entryways Building" that was planned by engineer Frank Gehry. While Microsoft had recently given monetary help to the organization, this was the main individual gift got from Gates.[168]

The Maxwell Dworkin Laboratory of the Harvard John A. Paulson School of Engineering and Applied Sciences is named after the moms of the two Gates and Microsoft President Steven A. Ballmer, both of whom were understudies (Ballmer was an individual from the school's graduating class of 1977, while Gates left his examinations for Microsoft), and gave assets for the research facility's construction.[169] Gates likewise gave $6 million to the development of the Gates Computer Science Building, finished in January 1996, on the grounds of Stanford University. The structure contains the Computer Science Department and the Computer Systems Laboratory (CSL) of Stanford's Engineering department.[170]

Beginning around 2005, Gates and his establishment have checked out taking care of worldwide disinfection issues. For instance, they reported the "Reexamine the Toilet Challenge", which has gotten significant media interest.[171] To bring issues to light for the subject of disinfection and potential arrangements, Gates drank water that was "delivered from human excrement" in 2014 – it was created from a sewage ooze treatment process called the Omni Processor.[172][173] In mid 2015, he likewise showed up with Jimmy Fallon on The Tonight Show and provoked him to check whether he could taste the distinction between this recycled water or packaged water.[174]

In November 2017, Gates said he would give $50 million to the Dementia Discovery Fund, an investment reserve that looks for treatment for Alzheimer's infection. He likewise promised an extra $50 million to fire up adventures working in Alzheimer's research.[175] Bill and Melinda Gates have said that they mean to leave their three youngsters $10 million each as their legacy. With just $30 million kept locked down, they are relied upon to part with around 99.96% of their wealth.[176] On August 25, 2018, Gates conveyed $600,000 through his establishment by means of UNICEF which is helping flood impacted casualties in Kerala, India.[177]

On April 29, 2017, Gates banded together with Swiss tennis legend Roger Federer in playing in the Match for Africa 4, a noncompetitive tennis match at a sold-out Key Arena in Seattle. The occasion was on the side of the Roger Federer Foundation's cause endeavors in Africa.[178] Federer and Gates played against John Isner, the highest level American player for a lot of this decade, and Mike McCready, the lead guitarist for Pearl Jam. The pair dominated the game 6 games to 4. By and large, they brought up $2 million for kids in Africa.[179] The next year, Gates and Federer got back to play in the Match for Africa 5 on March 5, 2018, at San Jose's SAP Center. Their rivals were Jack Sock, one of the top American players and a huge homerun champ in pairs, and Savannah Guthrie, a co-anchor for NBC's Today show. Doors and Federer recorded their second match triumph together by a score of 6–3 and the occasion raised more than $2.5 million.[180]

CHAPTER FIVE

Personal Life

> *"Most people overestimate what they can do in one year and underestimate what they can do in ten years."*

Doors is an eager peruser, and the roof of his huge home library is engraved with a citation from The Great Gatsby.[182] He likewise appreciates scaffold, tennis and golf.[183][184] His days are anticipated him on a moment by-minute premise, comparably to the U.S. president's schedule.[185] Despite his abundance and broad business travel, Gates flew standard class (economy class) in business airplane until 1997, when he purchased a private jet.[186]

Entryways bought the Codex Leicester, an assortment of logical compositions by Leonardo da Vinci, for US$30.8 million at a sale in 1994.[187] In 1998, he purportedly paid $30 million for the first 1885 oceanic work of art Lost on the Grand Banks, at the time a record cost for an American painting.[188] In 2016, he uncovered that he was shading blind.[189]

Doors wedded Melinda French on the Hawaiian Island of Lanai on January 1, 1994.[190] They met in 1987 after

Melinda started working at Microsoft.[191] At the hour of their marriage, Gates was given consent by Melinda to invest restricted energy with his ex, money manager Ann Winblad.[192] Bill and Melinda have three youngsters: Jennifer, Rory and Phoebe.[193] The family's home is an earth-shielded house in the side of a slope sitting above Lake Washington in Medina, Washington. In 2009, local charges on the manor were accounted for to be US$1.063 million, on a complete surveyed worth of US$147.5 million.[194] The 66,000-square-foot (6,100 m2) home has a 60-foot (18 m) pool with a submerged music framework, just as a 2,500-square-foot (230 m2) rec center and a 1,000-square-foot (93 m2) feasting room.[195] On May 3, 2021, the Gateses declared they had chosen to separate following 27 years of marriage and 34 years as a couple.[196] They said they would continue to cooperate on magnanimous efforts.[196][197] The Wall Street Journal revealed that Melinda had been meeting with separate from lawyers starting around 2019, refering to interviews that recommended Bill's binds with Jeffrey Epstein was something like one of her concerns.[198] The separation was concluded on August 2, 2021.[199]

A New York Times article announced that Gates' relationship with indicted sex wrongdoer Jeffrey Epstein began in 2011, only a couple of years after Epstein's conviction, and proceeded for certain years, remembering a visit to Epstein's home with Melinda for the fall of 2013, in spite of her proclaimed discomfort.[200] Gates said in 2011 with regards to Epstein: "His way of life is altogether different and sort of interesting despite the fact that it would not work for me".[201]

The profundity of the companionship among Gates and Epstein is indistinct. Entryways for the most part remarked about his relationship with Epstein that "I met him. I didn't have any business relationship or fellowship with him".[202] However, Gates visited Epstein "ordinarily, notwithstanding [Epstein's] past".[200] Gates took somewhere around one trip in 2013 in Epstein's notorious Lolita Express aircraft.[200]

It was accounted for that Epstein and Gates "examined the Gates Foundation and philanthropy".[200] However, in a meeting in 2019 Gates totally denied any association among Epstein and the Gates Foundation or his charity generally.[202] In August 2021, Gates said he had gatherings with Epstein because on the grounds that Gates trusted Epstein could give cash to altruistic work, however nothing happened to the thought. Entryways added, "It was a gigantic error to invest energy with him, to provide him with the believability of being there."[85]

It has likewise been accounted for that Epstein and Gates met with Nobel Committee seat Thorbjørn Jagland at his home in Strasbourg, France in March 2013 to examine the Nobel Prize.[203][204] Also in participation were agents of the International Peace Institute which has gotten millions in awards from the Gates Foundation, including a $2.5 million "local area commitment" award in October 2013.[205]

Entryways' public picture has changed throughout the long term. At first he was seen as a splendid however savage "looter nobleman", a "geek turned-tycoon".[206] Starting in 2000 with the establishment of the Bill and Melinda Gates Foundation, and especially after he ventured down as head of Microsoft, he directed his concentration toward altruism, spending more than $50 billion on causes like wellbeing, neediness, and instruction. His picture transformed "from overbearing technocrat to pious deliverer", a "huggable very rich person techno-humanitarian", celebrated on magazine covers and pursued for his perspectives on significant issues like worldwide wellbeing and environment change.[206] Still one more change in general assessment came in 2021 with the declaration that he and Melinda were separating. Inclusion of that continuing achieved out data heartfelt quests for ladies who worked for him, a drawn out extra-conjugal undertaking, and a companionship with indicted kid sex dealer Jeffrey Epstein.[201] This brought about a critical disintegration of his public picture. In June 2021, The New Republic depicted Gates as an "oligarch" and as "simply one more frightening rich guy".[207]

In a meeting with Rolling Stone, Gates said as to his confidence: "The ethical frameworks of religion, I believe, are really significant. We've brought our children up in a strict manner; they've gone to the Catholic church that Melinda goes to and I partake in. I've been extremely fortunate, and in this manner I owe it to attempt to diminish the imbalance on the planet. Furthermore that is somewhat of a strict conviction. That is to say, it's no less than a moral belief."[208] In a similar 2014 meeting he likewise said: "I concur with individuals like Richard Dawkins that humanity felt the requirement for creation fantasies. Before we truly started to get illness and the climate and things like that, we looked for bogus clarifications for them. Presently science has filled in a portion of the domain – not all – that religion used to fill. However, the secret and the magnificence of the world is predominantly astounding, and there's no logical clarification of how it occurred. To say that it was produced by irregular numbers, that appears, you know, kind of an uncharitable view [laughs]. I think it's a good idea to have confidence in God, however precisely what choice in your life you make contrastingly as a result of it, I don't know."[208]

In 1999, his abundance momentarily outperformed US$101 billion.[209][186] Since 2000, the ostensible worth of his Microsoft property has declined because of a fall in Microsoft's stock cost after the website bubble burst and the multi-billion dollar gifts he has made to his altruistic establishments. In May 2006, Gates commented that he wanted that he were not the most extravagant man on the planet since he despised the consideration it brought.[210] In March 2010, Gates was the second richest individual after Carlos Slim, however recaptured the top situation in 2013, as indicated by the Bloomberg Billionaires List.[211][212] Slim retook the position again in June 2014[213][214] (however at that point lost the top situation back to Gates). Somewhere in the range of 2009 and 2014, his abundance multiplied from US$40 billion to more than US$82 billion.[215] In October 2017, Gates was outperformed by Amazon organizer Jeff Bezos as the most extravagant individual in the world.[16] On November 15, 2019, he by and by turned into the most extravagant individual on the planet after a 48% increment in Microsoft shares, outperforming Bezos.[216] Gates told the BBC, "I've paid more expense than any individual ever, and happily so ... I've paid more than $6 billion in taxes."[217] He is a defender of higher charges, especially for the rich.[218]

Doors has held the best position on the rundown of The World's Billionaires for 18 out of the beyond 23 years.[219] Gates has a few speculations outside Microsoft, which in 2006 paid him a compensation of US$616,667 and US$350,000 reward totalling US$966,667.[220] In 1989, he established Corbis, an advanced imaging organization. In 2004, he turned into an overseer of Berkshire Hathaway, the venture organization headed by long-lasting companion Warren Buffett.[221]

In 1987, Gates was recorded as a tycoon in Forbes magazine's 400 Richest People in America issue, worth $1.25 billion at that point, and was the world's most youthful independent billionaire.[14] Since 1987, Gates has been remembered for the Forbes The World's Billionaires list and was the most well off individual from 1995 to 1996,[222] 1998 to 2007, 2009, and held the spot until 2018 preceding being overwhelmed by Jeff Bezos.[15] Gates was number one on the Forbes 400 rundown from 1993 through to 2007, 2009, and 2014 through 2017.[223][224]

CHAPTER SIX

Quotes

" *"I choose a lazy person to do a hard job. Because a lazy person will find an easy way to do it."*

"If you can't make it good, at least make it look good."

"Your most unhappy customers are your greatest source of learning."

"Most people overestimate what they can do in one year and underestimate what they can do in ten years."

"Success is a lousy teacher. It seduces smart people into thinking they can't lose."

"I really had a lot of dreams when I was a kid, and I think a great deal of that grew out of the fact that I had a chance to read a lot."

"If you give people tools, and they use their natural abilities and their curiosity, they will develop things in ways that will surprise you very much beyond what you might have expected."

"I agree with people like Richard Dawkins that mankind felt the need for creation myths. Before we really began to understand disease and the weather and things like that, we sought false explanations for them. Now science has filled in some of the realm – not all – that religion used to fill."

"DNA is like a computer program but far, far more advanced than any software ever created."

"As we look ahead into the next century, leaders will be those who empower others."

"

9 798885 301923

Printed by Libri Plureos GmbH in Hamburg,
Germany